MEDITATIONS ON CHRIST'S
WORDS FROM THE CROSS

Meditations on Christ's Words from the Cross

Gilbert Meilaender

With a Foreword by
Frank C. Senn

ALPB Books

Delhi, New York

The American Lutheran Publicity Bureau wishes to acknowledge and thank Gregory P. Fryer for his editorial assistance, Jeffery Neal Larson (www.commonrenderings.com) for the cover artwork, William Fensterer for his proofreading of the text and Dorothy Zelenko for typesetting and production.
Paul Robert Sauer
Executive Director

American Lutheran Publicity Bureau
P.O. Box 327
Delhi, New York 13753

ISBN 1-892921-28-6

Gilbert Meilaender, *Meditations on Christ's Words from the Cross*
Delhi, NY: ALPB Books, 2015.

Contents

Foreword

The last words of any person are treated with reverence. Even persons condemned to death in a criminal justice system are traditionally given an opportunity to make one last statement. All the more reverence, therefore, must be accorded to the last words of the One who was also condemned to death in a criminal justice system, however flawed, but whose followers believe he was the Son of God sent by God the Father to redeem his lost creatures from sin, death, and the power of the Evil One. Indeed, Mark the Evangelist has an executor of that system, a Roman centurion, proclaim what Jesus' own disciples failed to see, "Truly this man was God's Son" (Mark 15:39).

The four evangelists were careful to preserve the "last words" of Jesus on the cross and Christians have meditated on those "words"—seven statements in all—ever since. The first reported Good Friday three hour (Tre Ore) devotional service based on the seven last words of Christ was presented in Lima, Peru in 1732 by Father Alphonso Messia, SJ. From there it spread quickly throughout Latin America and was adopted by Protestants in North America.

It is a devotional service with an ecumenical appeal. The Tre Ore service is not typically observed in Europe, but musical reflections on these words are offered in oratorios and even in a string quartet by Franz Josef Haydn.

Two of the seven words are not the words of Jesus himself, but of Psalms 22:1 and 31:5. In his last hour Jesus the Jew turned to the hymnal of his people for appropriate words. The Fourth Evangelist says that Jesus' words "I thirst" were to fulfill the Scriptures— Psalm 69:21. Christians have seen the Old Testament scriptures fulfilled in Christ, but especially the psalms. What did Matthew and Mark intend by recording Jesus' utterance of the words of Psalm 22? Was it just a stark cry of dereliction? Mark was clear that Jesus was abandoned by his disciples: "they all fled". They didn't make it to the climax of his ministry. Did Jesus also feel that God had abandoned him? Or was this the incipit (the beginning) of the whole psalm, which ends in a note of praise and affirmation that this saving deed shall be proclaimed to a generation yet unborn? Did Matthew, whose gospel begins with the coming of the gentiles to worship the Messiah of Jews and ends with that Messiah's great commission to his apostles to make disciples of all nations, think in terms of the universal proclamation of the saving event of the cross in Jesus' use of this psalm of lament and praise?

These thoughts tease exegesis. But the words of Jesus in Luke and John are in conformity with the story of Jesus as told by those evangelists. Luke's story of Jesus emphasizes the Master's authority to forgive sins and to reach out to marginalized people, like the so-called "repentant thief," to whom Jesus promises paradise "today". John sees "the hour" of the cross as the whole purpose of Jesus' mission. At the cross he provides for his apostles (represented by the beloved disciple) to care for his church (represented by his Mother) and declares victory ("It is finished") after fulfilling the Scriptures with the words "I thirst". This note of triumph makes Good Friday "good," or actually "God's Friday," and the traditional Gospel in the Good Friday Liturgy is the Passion according to St. John.

In the order of the words as usually followed in the Three Hour Devotion, "It is finished" is the penultimate word. The "last word" is Jesus' use of Psalm 31:5 in Luke's Passion: "Father, into your hands I commend my spirit." These are our last words also at the end of the day and at the end of life. They form the Responsory to the Lesson in the Office of Compline: "Into your hands,

O Lord, I commend my spirit; you have redeemed me, O Lord God of truth. Glory to the Father and to the Son and to the Holy Spirit."

This brings us to the use we make of these words. They connect with our everyday lives; indeed, our everyday lives are absorbed into the redeeming work of Christ and thereby transformed. Well does the preacher or teacher probe the various dimensions and realities of human life, both individual and social, to offer up examples of all the aspects of life that can be redeemed and transfigured by the cross of Christ. The noted Lutheran teacher, Gilbert Meilaender, does just that. As he ponders the historical and social context of the sufferings of Christ, he also probes the historical and social contexts of human suffering in its various aspects. He is eminently qualified to bring together human situations and the cross of Christ, having taught Christian ethics for many years at Oberlin College and now at Valparaiso University. Dr. Meilaender has been a faithful teacher of the church in conversation with the world throughout his career, and we are indebted to him for offering us not one, but two, sets of meditations on the seven last words of Christ, holy words of our Savior spoken to us and for us.

Frank C. Senn, STS

Preface

On Good Friday, from noon to three o'clock, some Christian congregations mark the three hours Jesus suffered on the cross with what is called a *Tre Ore* (three hour) service. Although there is no single set form that such a service must follow, quite often it incorporates meditations on the seven different sayings of Jesus from the cross, as those are recorded in the several gospels.

The fourteen meditations in this small volume, two on each of Jesus' seven "last words," were first written for use in such a liturgical setting. One might also, however, use them simply for personal meditation and reflection. In either case, my aim here is not to worry about the particular emphases of each of the Gospels but, rather, to reflect on the meaning of the cross for Christian belief, practice, and piety.

The First Word (i)

"Father, forgive them, for they know not what they do."

> *Jesus, I will ponder now,*
> *On your holy passion. . . .*
> *Make me see your great distress,*
> *Anguish and affliction,*
> *Bonds and stripes and wretchedness*
> *And your crucifixion.*

And the wonder of it is that, when we ponder that anguish and affliction, that great distress, the *first* word we hear from the crucified one is: "Father, forgive them; for they know not what they do." Forgive whom?

+ Forgive the soldiers – They're tough men, hardened by the burdens they've borne sustaining Rome's far-flung empire. They know how quickly disorder can break out if they don't do their job swiftly and effectively. And so, in the service of that great good, the public order, which cannot be sustained without them, they crucify the Lord of Glory.

+ Forgive Pilate – The little we know of him from other sources suggests that he was probably in over his head as Roman Procurator of Judea. Sent from Rome to try to govern people whom he did not understand very well and who were constantly unhappy and restless under Roman rule. Struggling as best he could—within the limits of his understanding and ability—to maintain a very fragile peace. And so, in the service of that great good, and there are few goods greater than peace, Pilate sentences to crucifixion the Lord of Glory.

+ Forgive the chief priests – They were Sadducees, who could not have been very sympathetic to some aspects of this rabbi Jesus' teaching. But still, he was a fellow Jew, and they turned against him only because they thought they had to for the sake of the whole people. They knew how dangerous it would be to bring down Rome's wrath upon tiny Judea. And so, in the service of that great good, the survival of God's chosen people, they urge crucifixion of the Lord of Glory.

+ Forgive the other leaders of the people – Deeply pious Jews, they were sincerely committed to following as best they could the way of life God had given Israel to mark her out as his holy people. And that very way of life, which came from God, seemed to compel them to consider Jesus a blasphemer. "We have a law," as they say in John's Gospel (19:7), God's law, "and by that law he ought to die." And so, in the service of that great good, obedience to Israel's God, they support the crucifixion of the Lord of Glory.

They didn't know what they were doing. All of them, in their different ways, trying to accomplish something good. And it is the deep mystery—even, in some ways, the offense—of sin, that its roots lie in the desire to do good. All these people trying to make things work out right—and what a mess they made of it. "Father, forgive them," Jesus says.

> *Yet, O Lord, not thus alone*
> *Make me see your passion. . . .*
> *For I also and my sin*
> *Wrought your deep affliction;*
> *This the shameful cause has been*
> *Of your crucifixion.*

How similarly rooted in our own love for what is good are the sins that wrought Jesus's deep affliction. Forgive *us.*

+ Caring for our children – and wanting so much to help them succeed—and often in over our heads at that task. Sometimes pushing too hard, other times giving too much freedom. And so, in the service of that great good, their happiness, forgetting that only God can guarantee that happiness.

+ Loving our parents – and caring so much about them that we cannot accept in them the weaknesses and failings we so easily excuse in others. And so, in the service of that great good, the special affection we have for them, failing to honor them as God's representatives before us.

+ Wanting to be friendly toward others – not wishing to alienate them by making a point of disagreements or insisting on being different. And so, in the service of that great good, and there are few goods greater than friendship, turning aside from Jesus and the different way of life to which he calls us.

+ Trying to carry out our work efficiently and productively – hoping to leave behind a legacy of accomplishment. And so, in the service of that great good, important goals we have set for ourselves and the institutions we serve, overriding all too often the claims and needs of others, in whom we ought to see the face of Christ.

Forgive us.

All of us, in our different ways, aiming at something good. All of us, in our different ways, trying to make things work out right—and, all too often, making a mess of it. Helping to crucify the Lord of Glory.

And, therefore, of us also, and for us also, Jesus speaks from the cross. Luke writes: "Jesus said, 'Father, forgive them; for they know not what they do.'" And in fact, it would be perfectly accurate to translate Luke just a little differently, to translate it this way as a continuing action: "Jesus kept on saying, 'Father, forgive them; for they know not what they do.'" On this Good Friday we can and should make it a present tense: Jesus *keeps on saying*.

This is not a word spoken only once with reference to soldiers, Roman governor, leaders of the people. It is a word repeated. It is a prayer of forgiveness that echoes through the centuries. A prayer for the countless generations of humanity—for all of us—who want so much to accomplish something good, and who can't seem to get it right. "I also and my sin / Wrought your deep affliction."

In the face of that failure, our failure—day after day, year after year—the crucified Jesus keeps on saying of and for each of us: "Father, forgive them; for they know not what they do."

The First Word (ii)

"Father, forgive them, for they know not what they do."

Part of the mystery of Good Friday is that we come to stand beneath Jesus' cross and, strange as it may seem, this place of suffering is a place where sorrows are healed. As a Lenten hymn puts it:

> *Beneath the cross of Jesus*
> *I long to take my stand;*
> *The shadow of a mighty rock*
> *Within a weary land,*
> *A home within a wilderness,*
> *A rest upon the way,*
> *From the burning of the noontide heat*
> *And burdens of the day.*

And as we take our own stand beneath this cross, the first word we hear from the crucified one is a word that heals: "Father, forgive them, for they know not what they do."

Read most naturally, these words refer first of all to the soldiers doing the crucifying. Hard men, accustomed to the brutal work needed to sustain Rome's far-flung empire, they don't make judgments about guilt and innocence. They just carry out their orders—swiftly, efficiently, and, no doubt, harshly. They probably don't worry too much about the larger significance of what they're doing.

But, of course, there are also others who stand behind them, who are at least as responsible for what takes place on Calvary: the Roman governor Pilate, the chief priests and other leaders of the people. They think they know what they're doing. In their different ways, and from their different perspectives, they're buying some peace and order. They're keeping the lid on political passions that can flare up at any moment. They too, however, cannot know the full significance of what they do.

We would not, however, gather here today to ponder Jesus' holy passion if these were the only actors in the story, the only ones for whom Jesus prays in this first word from the cross that Luke records. No, this is a story in which we too have a part, and it is a blessing for us that we do.

There is a Jewish philosopher named Michael Wyschogrod, a quite elderly man by now, and a very fine scholar who has written important and, indeed, profound essays about Jewish-Christian relations. A few years ago I was at a meeting in which Wyschogrod, who lives in New York City, was also a participant. And at one point he told a story, which, at least on his telling, went like this:

He and his wife were riding the subway and had gotten off at (I think it was) the 181ˢᵗ St. exit. It's an exit that is quite deep underground, and you have to ride an elevator up to ground level. The elevator was packed with people, and Wyschogrod and his wife—both quite elderly—were almost the last people on. Just after them, and the very last person to squeeze in at the last second before the door closed, was a rather wild-looking and disheveled man, clearly somewhat drunk.

The door closed, and the elevator began to ascend. The man turned to Wyschogrod (who would, of course, have been wearing his yarmulke, which would clearly identify him as Jewish). The man turned to him and said rather loudly, "Why did you Jews kill our Lord?"

And Wyschogrod replied: "It wasn't only the Jews. It was all of us, all of our sins, that killed Jesus." To which the man said, "yes, that's true." And other people on the elevator broke out in agreement. "Yes, all of us, all our sins, we drove the nails into his hands."

It would be good if all Christians were as ready with the right response as this Jewish philosopher was. For surely it was all of us, all our sins, that killed Jesus. And terrible as that truth may be, it is only when we see it— only when, like the crowd in the elevator, we say, "yes, it was all of us"—that we take our stand beneath the cross of Jesus. Then we join the soldiers, the Roman governor, the leaders of the people—and Jesus says of us too, "Father, forgive them." For these two things go together in the Good Friday story—the truth of our own unworthiness, and the wonder of God's healing love in Jesus.

Because they go together, this is not just somebody else's story. This is our story. We too don't quite know what we're doing. We can't sort out the many ways in which, often without bothering to think about it, we are just a few more soldiers, driving the nails into the hands of the very God whom we need and whom we want to be present with us.

We spend our lives reaching out for something we can't quite describe. We may call it peace, joy, love, acceptance—it's not easy to find the right words. But we can't seem to make it happen. We can't find a way to push the door open into the room that contains whatever it is we're after.

The healing meaning of Good Friday is that the door opens only from the inside, and that Jesus has been willing to put his shoulder to that door and open it. "Father, forgive them," he says of us. Here at Calvary, where good and evil meet and cross each other, we get a glimpse of the very heart of God, the forgiving heart that is the center of the universe. Here there is welcome for all who don't really know what they're doing—the soldiers, Pilate, the chief priests, you and me. None of us worthy. All of us invited in.

That's what it means that we have a part in this story and can say in the words of the hymn:

> *Upon the cross of Jesus,*
> *My eye at times can see*
> *The very dying form of one*
> *Who suffered there for me.*
> *And from my contrite heart, with tears,*
> *Two wonders I confess:*
> *The wonder of his glorious love*
> *And my unworthiness.*

The Second Word (i)

"Truly I say to you, today you will be with me in paradise."

What language shall I borrow
To thank thee, dearest friend,
For this thy dying sorrow,
Thy pity without end?

That question, from one of the great Lenten hymns, should be ours today: "What language shall I borrow / to thank thee, dearest friend?"

What is it that we can say on this Good Friday to the One whom we call Lord, but who hangs on the cross, with thorns his only crown? What can we say to express our thanks for the gift of his life that Jesus here offers us?

Perhaps we can learn something from Dysmas—the name traditionally given to the man called the "penitent thief," who hangs on his own cross alongside Jesus.

"Remember me when you come into your kingdom," he says. We're so accustomed to his words that we may almost forget just how strange they are. This tough and hardened man, quite possibly a political insurrectionist, who, so far as we know, had never known Jesus or heard him, and who—even if he had ever heard Jesus—does not seem to have changed his behavior or the course of his life as a result . . . all of a sudden he says this? What was he thinking? What could he possibly have meant?

Did he really care about a Christ, a Messiah? And if he did, could he possibly have figured out that the messianic kingdom Jesus brings would not be one to overthrow Roman rule, but one that—as Jesus said to Pilate—is not a normal political kingdom of this world? If even Jesus' closest disciples didn't really understand this until after Jesus was raised, how can we suppose that Dysmas had it all figured out and wanted a place in that spiritual kingdom?

Perhaps a very different angle on Dysmas can give us the words we need today, the language we can borrow to express our thanks.

More than seventy years ago, in 1943, a series of twelve radio plays written by Dorothy L. Sayers was published under the title, *The Man Born to be King.* These plays had first been broadcast by the BBC in Great Britain in 1941-42. They tell the story of Jesus from birth to death and resurrection, but they tell the story with the imagination and insight that only a literary artist such as Sayers could bring.

Almost nowhere in the twelve plays is that imaginative insight more evident—or more striking—than in the way Sayers conveys the short little encounter between these two thieves, Gestas and Dysmas, and Jesus, crucified between them.

Jesus is mocked by the bystanders around the cross, and Gestas joins in. We need not pause to criticize Gestas, the man often called simply the "impenitent thief." Who can say what we would have done in his circumstances? Who knows what we might have said out of the depths of such pain and suffering?

But Dysmas was also suffering. Yet, what he does, as Sayers tells the story, is nothing short of amazing. In the midst of his own agony, he does what he can to comfort Jesus in his.

In Sayers' play it is not so much Dysmas' faith as his love that is central. He's no fool, and he thinks, as he says in the play, that Jesus must be "looney" if he imagines himself divine. But, still, he goes along with the game, trying to make Jesus feel better. You're all right, he says. This is just a bad dream, isn't it. Of course, one of these days you'll show up in a cloud of glory and astonish 'em all.

And then, wanting simply to humor—and thereby help—this poor, deluded man crucified beside him, he says very respectfully to Jesus, pretending that he speaks to a king: "Sir, you'll remember me, won't you, when you come into your kingdom?" To which Jesus makes his well-known reply that we ponder again today.

Dysmas' words are an act not so much of faith in a messianic deliverer as of concern for this man who is being mocked in his suffering. He seems to know almost instinctively what Jesus once taught: that the love shown to those who are least among us is love shown to Jesus.

Somehow, out of his own pain, Dysmas finds the strength to show to Jesus simple human kindness, which Jesus immediately recognizes as such. "Today you will be with me." That is to say, the kindness you thought you were offering to a harmless, deranged man, is really more than you know. It is kindness and love offered to the One to whom all our love must finally be directed.

Now, of course, we need not read the story in this way, in the imaginative way Sayers does. But if we do, it provides an answer to the question the hymn posed for us: What language shall I borrow, / to thank thee, dearest friend?"

We can borrow Dysmas' language, the language of love. Whatever we may be experiencing at this time in our life—whatever pain and suffering may have come our way—whatever crosses we may be given to carry—however puzzled we may sometimes be by this Jesus hanging on the cross—however hard we may find it to understand what God is doing there—we can still borrow Dysmas' language, the language of love: "Jesus, remember me when you come into your kingdom." We can pray in words the hymn also gave us:

Oh, make me thine forever,
And should I fainting be,
Lord, let me never, never
Outlive my love to thee.

Dysmas, it seems, did not outlive his love to Jesus. And we may be sure that, when we make his words our own, Jesus will respond to us as he did to Dysmas: "Today you will be with me in Paradise."

The Second Word (ii)

"Truly I say to you, today you will be with me in paradise."

In Westwood Cemetery in Oberlin, Ohio, there is an area known as "Missionary Rest." Buried there are some of the Oberlin missionaries to China from the late nineteenth century. On the marker at the gravesite of a young child of one of those missionaries are these simple words: "Dear Jesus, you know I love you. Take me to yourself."

As we stand today with Christians everywhere, looking with wonder—and perhaps a certain amount of incomprehension—at God dying on a cross, we may not know what we should say. One of the greatest hymns of Jesus' passion, "O Sacred Head Now Wounded," expresses our uncertainty: "What language shall I borrow / To thank thee, dearest friend?"

What language shall I borrow? This is no time to try to be creative. In the face of the mystery of this cross, we do well if we can learn from a condemned and dying criminal to say something about as simple as the words on that child's grave: "Dear Jesus, you know I love you. Take me to yourself."

Luke's Gospel has given us good reason to love this Jesus, who now is crucified. He has forgiven the sinful woman who washed his feet and dried them with her hair. He has healed the servant of that Roman centurion, even though he might seem to have no reason to care about a Roman soldier—a comrade of those who now crucify him. He has provided an image of the kind of love God shows us and would have us show in the story of the Good Samaritan. He has healed lepers, most of whom just forgot to come back and say thank-you. He has honored the meager offering of that widow who had only two copper coins to give to the temple treasury. He has painted the unforgettable picture of that father, waiting for his prodigal son to come home, and eager to celebrate when he does. But now, at the cross, his love and concern is hard pressed to find a fitting response. Very few seem brave enough or compassionate enough to show this dying man simple kindness.

St. Luke distinguishes for us three different responses from those who gather around the cross. There are some who find words to say, but, alas, they use words in order to taunt a suffering man. The leaders of the people mock Jesus: "He saved others; himself he cannot save." The Roman soldiers react in a similar taunting manner: "If you are the King of the Jews, save yourself." And one of the crucified thieves joins in. "Are you not the Christ? Save yourself and us."

We don't really want to be part of this first group. We would not knowingly or willingly join those people in their taunting, even if sometimes our lives may seem to mock any claim Christ might make upon us. If on occasion we seem to belong to this first group, this is the time when we should admit our shame and refuse any longer to be among the mockers.

There is also a second kind of response from those gathered near the cross. Their leaders may have scoffed, but of the rest of the people Luke says: They "stood by watching." Silent. Uncertain what to say. Needing borrowed language to give expression to feelings they were unable to articulate. And we may be like them: silent, but in search of words. Looking for someone to teach us how to go beyond silence, how to say what we need to say as we look at this cross.

From whom can we find language to borrow? Who can teach us that third possible response? Luke sets before us an exemplar. This teacher is no scholar. He is not even an especially good man. Luke calls him a thief, and, in fact, he was probably an insurrectionist and a cutthroat. Quite possibly he is one who deserved the punishment he was suffering on his own cross. Yet, without, it seems, the benefit of having been taught, he prays essentially the same prayer Jesus had taught his disciples to pray.

This crucified thief says, "Your kingdom come, Lord." He says what Luther says in his *Small Catechism's* explanation of the second petition of the Lord's Prayer: God's kingdom comes indeed without our prayer, but we pray in this petition that it may come to us also.

"Jesus," this thief says, "when you come into your kingdom—whenever that may be, wherever it may be— remember me." Let your kingdom come, even and also to me. Luke tells us nothing about how this dying thief reacted to Jesus' reply, but Christian imagination has filled in the gaps. William Cowper's well-known hymn, which pictures the blood flowing from Jesus's body as a cleansing flood, discerned in Jesus' response reason for joy: "The dying thief rejoiced to see / That fountain in his day."

If we are looking for language to borrow, looking for someone from whom to learn what we ought to say in the face of the unspeakable mystery of the cross, then this dying thief is one from whom we can learn to say something as simple as "remember me." "Dear Jesus, you know I love you. Take me to yourself."

And then Jesus speaks to us also. To all who find such words to pray—to each of us, as to that thief—Jesus says: "Today you will be with me in paradise." And we can then say in the words of Cowper's hymn:

> *Dear dying Lamb, thy precious blood*
> *Shall never lose its power,*
> *Till all the ransomed ones of God*
> *Be saved to sin no more.*

The Third Word (i)

"Woman, behold your son! Son, behold your mother!"

The hymn writer Thomas Pollock, who lived in the last half of the nineteenth century, composed a series of brief hymns on the seven words of Jesus spoken from the cross. The whole composition has been titled, "Jesus, In Your Dying Woes," and the three short stanzas on the third word from the cross give us a way to ponder that word's significance. These three short stanzas become our own Good Friday prayer. We can think about each of them in turn.

Jesus, loving to the end
Her whose heart Your sorrows rend,
And Your dearest human friend:
Hear us, holy Jesus.

I suppose it is not really a surprise that we should find both Jesus' mother and his closest friend (usually identified as the disciple John) near the cross. After all these people are connected to Jesus by the ties that we generally value most in life—ties of family and friendship. And certainly they belong there; for they were very close to this dying man.

But if such natural human ties are what qualify someone to stand near Jesus' cross, then it will be a very slim crowd indeed. In fact, it's not clear on what basis we ourselves would then draw near. And so the first thing we should perhaps remind ourselves is that this Jesus who is, as the hymn says, "loving to the end," loves far more widely and generously than we often do.

After all, this is his third word from the cross. There has already been a first word—forgiving those who torment and crucify him, accepting their presence at the cross. There has already been a second word—spoken to that crucified thief, who was probably more a revolutionary cutthroat than a mere thief. Jesus, loving to the end, has already admitted this thief into the fellowship of those who are near to him in his suffering.

So then, whatever gets someone into the company of those who come near to Jesus today, it is evidently not any claim we can make for ourselves, not any of the natural ties of family and friendship that we understandably value so highly. If not that, then what?

How, then, should we draw near? Consider the second stanza.

May we in Your sorrows share,
For Your sake all peril dare,
And enjoy Your tender care:
Hear us, holy Jesus.

There is a puzzling detail in the few verses in which John records this third word of Jesus. He describes Mary and the other women, and the disciple whom Jesus especially loves, as "standing by the cross." But Luke's Gospel (23:49) says that the women and others who had followed Jesus "stood at a distance and saw these things."

We don't know exactly what happened at Calvary, of course, nor just how the ordeal played out. But some people have conjectured that, although standing at a distance, John and Mary and some of the other women had come closer for a time during that three-hour period of darkness. It's only a guess, but there's something about it that rings true. If so, there may be a lesson in it for us.

When is it that we draw nearest to the crucified Jesus and, as the hymn puts it, enjoy his tender care? Perhaps it is when we find ourselves in the dark, uncertain about where we are headed or how to see what lies ahead— even fearful of what may lie before us. When, like Mary at the cross, we lose someone to whom we are very close.

When we are estranged from someone who has been a close friend. When the plans we had for the future have gone awry, and nothing seems to be working out the way we had hoped or expected. Perhaps we come closest to Jesus in our own moments of darkness. At any rate, isn't that what we prayed for in the hymn? "May we in Your sorrows share"—and in that way draw near?

This means that all who in their own darkness draw near to the crucified One are brought together into a new company, a new fellowship—as the hymn puts it in its third stanza.

> *May we all Your loved ones be,*
> *All one holy family,*
> *Loving since Your love we see:*
> *Hear us, holy Jesus.*

Very near the beginning of Jesus' ministry, as John's Gospel records it, Jesus had come to a wedding at Cana in Galilee. When the hosts ran out of wine to serve the guests, Jesus' mother had suggested that he do something about it. His answer to her probably always strikes us as a bit abrupt. "Woman," Jesus said, "my hour has not yet come."

We might say that what Jesus did at Cana was make clear that his mother, as his natural mother, had no essential role in the work he was to do. For, as his natural mother—a woman like Eve, whom Genesis calls the mother of all the living—Mary would not be a central player in what he was up to.

But now, at the cross, she is given a new and different role. Now she is once again "woman"—not as his natural mother, however, but as the new Eve, mother of a new humanity: the church, which is a new fellowship. "Here is your son," Jesus says to her. "Here is your mother," he says to John. Out of the darkness around the cross Jesus forms a new family, a family that drinks not the wine served at Cana, but the new wine that flows from Jesus' sword-pierced side.

It would be strange—and, in fact, inappropriate—if, when we sat around the family dinner table at home, husbands, wives, fathers, mothers, sons, and daughters simply called each other "brother" and "sister." That wouldn't quite fit. But when we come to the table where the new wine is served, that is exactly what we are. We come not as those connected by the natural ties of marriage, family, and friendship, but as what we might call single people—brothers and sisters in the new family God creates in the darkness around the cross.

Here today at Calvary God begins anew; he starts over. He forms a new family, a new company—brothers and sisters who draw near in the darkness to Jesus. And so we pray today:

> *May we all Your loved ones be,*
> *All one holy family,*
> *Loving, since Your love we see:*
> *Hear us holy Jesus.*

The Third Word (ii)

"Woman, behold your son! Son, behold your mother!"

This is not the way life is supposed to work—that the mother should outlive her son and have to watch him die. No, he is supposed to be at her side when she nears death—to care for her in her weakness as she once cared for him in his.

There's so much here—in this scene at Calvary—that seems out of kilter. An innocent man is being executed. Almost all his friends have run away, and one has actually handed him over to his enemies. He's dying the death reserved for criminals—although, whatever exactly he is, it isn't that (as even Pilate had sensed, when he found no guilt in him).

And now, his own mother, who once carried him within her and held him in her arms, can only watch him die. So much is out of kilter. We might find it a little hard to believe that God is at work in what's happening here.

And yet, the very next verse in John's Gospel, the verse that comes immediately after Jesus' words to Mary and John, begins: "After this, Jesus, knowing that all was now finished . . . ."

Everything finished—the last task done. Jesus had handed his mother and the beloved disciple over to each other, and that, evidently, completed the work his Father had given him to do. That the mother should watch her son die may be contrary to our sense of what is fitting, but somehow it was evidently part and parcel of God's plan—of the work Jesus had been sent to carry out.

Jesus may be leaving them, but he has this one last task: to establish the community he leaves behind (for that is what Mary and the disciple really represent here). They form in miniature the community we have come to call the church, for which Jesus here makes clear his lasting and abiding concern.

That, of course, is the reason Christians still gather on Good Friday to meditate upon this scene at Calvary. It is God's doing, the Father's plan and will. To see what Jesus does here, to listen to the words he speaks to his mother and the disciple, to hear them as words spoken also to us, is to look upon the face of God and see love.

The Scottish theologian Thomas Torrance tells in one of his books how, as a young army chaplain, he had once held the hand of a dying 19-year-old soldier. And how then again, years later, as a pastor in Aberdeen, he had held the hand of the oldest woman in his congregation as she lay dying. And both of them, he writes—separated by so many years and such different life experiences—both of them had asked him exactly the same question: "Is God really like Jesus?" Is God really like this man stretched out on the cross, remembering his mother and his disciple. And Torrance had assured them that God is indeed like that. To hear the voice of Jesus reaching into our own lives, counting us among those disciples whom (even on the cross) he remembers, is to hear the voice of God: Immanuel, God with us.

"Woman, behold your son." "Son, behold your mother." Having said that—having demonstrated to the very end his care for those who had followed him, and for the community of followers he would leave behind, Jesus' work was finished. But ours was only begun, for the community Jesus names here at the cross, the community that will be enlivened on Easter morning, must learn to share in his sufferings and to entrust itself, as he did, to the Father's keeping.

Thus, the *Stabat Mater*, the medieval poem meditating on the sorrow of Mary at the cross, envisions us drawn into a suffering shared with her.

> *Jesus, may her deep devotion*
> *Stir in me the same emotion,*
> *Source of love, redeemer true.*
> *Let me thus, fresh ardor gaining*
> *And a purer love attaining,*
> *Consecrate my life to you.*

That is the work the crucified Jesus hands over to us today and asks us to nourish in each other—a willingness to share in his sorrows and a quest for holiness, for that purer love.

Usually we think—and rightly enough—of bringing our burdens here and laying them beneath the cross for Jesus to carry. We come to Calvary in our weakness and vulnerability in order to do that, and Jesus does not disappoint us. He bears those burdens.

Nevertheless, we also pick up new burdens at this cross. Jesus finishes his work in the world precisely by placing into our hands the task of continuing it. Having done what his Father sent him to do, having shown us once and for all what God is like, having carried the burdens we bring to him, he reaches down into our out-of-kilter world to remember us . . . and to make us his hands and voice in that world.

To see Jesus' cross in this way is to see that he is at his mother's side, and every believer's side, in the moment of death. He is there when we are there, when we bring his word of mercy and love, the word that makes him present.

On this Good Friday he once again asks us to take up the task he gives us and learn to respond as Mary, his mother, had years earlier, when the angel brought her that unexpected news that she would carry God in our world: "I am the servant of the Lord. Let it be to me according to your word."

The Fourth Word (i)

"My God, my God, why have you forsaken me?"

Years ago, in some long-since forgotten place, I read about a little boy who was looking at a picture book, learning for the first time the story of Jesus. He came at last to the picture of the crucifixion itself. He looked long and thoughtfully at the scene depicted there—the crown of thorns, the spear, the nails, the torso stretched out on that cross. Finally, having taken it all in, he turned the page and said, "If God had been there, he would not have let them do it."

And yet, the mystery of it all, the mystery is that God *was* there—and God let them do it.

What are we to make of that mystery? Of the seven last words of Christ, perhaps of all the words in the Bible, there can be very few that invite our speculation more than Jesus' cry of abandonment: "My God, my God, why have you forsaken me?" His cry invites us, and in some ways seduces us, to try to figure out how it could be that God could be abandoned by God.

In the mystery of the love that the Father has for his Son from eternity, which love the Son from eternity offers back to his Father through the bond of their Spirit, in the mystery of that never-ending and unconquerable *presence* to each other in love, the Father is *absent* from his beloved Son at the cross.

We puzzle over "how" that could be, but notice that Jesus does not. His question is not "how?" but "why?" That one Hebrew word—*lama*—is the saddest word of all in this story. "Why?"

If the question is "how" God can abandon God, then let us be honest: We cannot penetrate this mystery and give an answer. But if the question is "why," we may at least know where to start. For the mystery begins not with God abandoning this man on the cross, but with man abandoning God. "O my people," says the Lord, "why have you forsaken me?" All the generations of unfaithful humanity—both Israel and the nations—are gathered together in this one man, upon whom their unfaithfulness is laid.

Why did we do it? Why abandon God? Because we preferred to do things our own way. Because we were afraid to place our hope in God. Because we were weak when strength was needed, fearful when courage was needed, blind when sight was needed, confident of ourselves when humility was needed. "O my people, why have *you* forsaken *me*?" The cry of abandonment is, first of all, God's own anguished cry, when we turn away from the One who has loved us from all eternity.

We have forsaken him, and it is therefore no surprise that he should seem absent just when we most need his presence. This has often been the sad experience of the generations of men and women in countless times and places: that God may seem to vanish from us in our time of greatest need. The confidence we thought we had in God is suddenly blown away, and we are left, it seems, entirely on our own to face our troubles. And, therefore, if in Jesus God has come to be one of us, to share our life fully and completely, why then, of course, he must also share this seeming absence of God in his time of need.

When we experience God's absence, that word "why"— *lama*—becomes our cry also. Why have I fallen ill? Why am I dying? Why is this one whom I love so dearly ill or dying? Why has my child not spoken to me for years? Why has my son been using drugs? Why is there no money to pay the bills? Why did my husband—or my wife—leave me? Why can't I find a way to set right that cruel word I spoke? Why can't I take back what I did so thoughtlessly in a foolish moment? Why isn't God here to make it all better?

All those "whys"—yours, mine, and those of generations long gone—are gathered and piled in a heap at this cross.

All of it amounting to what the little boy instinctively thought: "If God had been there, he would not have let them do it." Why aren't you present here, God?

And, therefore, in order to be present, to be God with us—to be Immanuel—Jesus must experience the absence of God in his time of greatest need. Only in God's absence *from* Jesus can God be present *with* us *in* Jesus.

How God has done this we will never quite fathom. But that he has done it means that we can stop asking "why?" We can be confident that Jesus was the last human being who ever needs to feel completely abandoned by God. After this cross, we are never alone. We can look on pictures of the crucifixion not with horror or bewilderment, but with gratitude. God has been absent from Jesus so that in this same Jesus God may be present with us—present here, where we so often seem forsaken and abandoned.

On Good Friday, then, we can pray as the hymn gives us fitting word:

> *Therefore, kind Jesus, since I cannot pay thee,*
> *I do adore thee, and will ever pray thee;*
> *Think on thy pity and thy love unswerving,*
> *Not my deserving.*

The Fourth Word (ii)

"My God, my God, why have you forsaken me?"

Many of you probably know the book called *The Lion, the Witch, and the Wardrobe*. It is the very first of C.S. Lewis's Chronicles of Narnia. In that story, the great lion Aslan rescues Edmund from the White Witch. Edmund has been a traitor, and part of the very structure of Narnia, the order that keeps life in place, is that traitors belong to the Witch. She has a right to their lives. That is the deep magic from the dawn of time, woven into the fabric of Narnia when it was first created and carved into the Stone Table.

Aslan cannot disagree. He knows that by right Edmund's life is now forfeited to the Witch, and Narnia cannot survive if this truth is not honored. But he strikes a bargain with the Witch, a bargain that she greedily and foolishly accepts. He will take Edmund's place. He will forfeit his life to her so that Edmund can go free.

And if you know the story, you know what happens then. In the darkness of that night, when he has left all his friends and companions behind, Aslan is put to death by the Witch and her followers at the Stone Table. But when morning comes—with Susan and Lucy watching—the Stone Table cracks down the middle and Aslan comes back to life. No more darkness. No more loneliness. Instead, he takes Susan and Lucy on a wild romp through Narnia.

He tells them that, though the Witch had known the deep magic from the dawn of time, she did not know an even deeper magic from before the dawn of time—a magic not just written into the order of Narnia, but a magic that was written into the very character of the Emperor beyond the Sea.

What was that deeper magic? It was that if one who was not a traitor willingly offered his life for the sake of the traitor, then the Stone Table would crack and death would begin to work backwards. The darkness and desolation of the Stone Table did not have the last word. On the other side of that darkness was light and life, joy and celebration.

And if we turn now to this fourth word of Jesus spoken on the cross—"My God, my God, why have you forsaken me?"—we will not go wrong if we think of it a little bit like that story in *The Lion, the Witch, and the Wardrobe.*

Jesus didn't just make up this cry of anguish. He didn't create it out of his own imagination. Jesus was a faithful Israelite, and he knew the scriptures of his people. In particular, he knew the psalms, prayers that the people of Israel had been praying individually and collectively for centuries. "My God, my God, why have you forsaken me?" are words that begin the 22nd Psalm. That psalm gives people who feel alone and forsaken words they can use to ask God for help. They are words that must have come naturally to Jesus in such a time of need, and they are words that can teach us something important today.

Matthew tells us that the people around the cross misunderstood Jesus. When he said "Eli, Eli"—"my God, my God"—they thought he was calling for Elijah to come and help him. And in our own way, a different way, we too might misunderstand this terrible cry of Jesus. We could forget to notice that little pronoun "my."

Yes, Jesus feels alone and forsaken—forsaken even by the God of Israel. Yes, in some way too mysterious for us to understand, the incarnate Son of the Father is experiencing the absence of his Father. All that is true. But we would misunderstand if we think of Jesus as simply having despaired here, of having lost all hope in Israel's God.

For he continues to claim this God as his own—as "my" God. In the midst of suffering that is physical, emotional, and spiritual—suffering that we cannot really imagine or comprehend—in the midst of that he somehow clings to God. And it is that same psalm, the 22ⁿᵈ Psalm, that gives us words to do so:

> My God, my God, why hast thou forsaken me?
>> Why art thou so far from helping me,
>> from the words of my groaning?
> O my God, I cry by day, but thou dost not answer;
>> and by night, but find no rest.
> Yet thou art holy,
>> enthroned on the praises of Israel.
> In thee our fathers trusted;
>> they trusted, and thou didst deliver them.
> To thee they cried, and were saved;
>> in thee they trusted, and were not disappointed.

This is not a promise that things will always go well with us. It is not a gospel of health and happiness. But it is a promise that, come what may and however desolate and abandoned we may feel, each can still call out to Israel's God, the Father of Jesus, as "my" God. He will not forget us. He will say to us as he said to Israel through the prophet Hosea:

> How can I give you up, O Ephraim!
>> How can I hand you over, O Israel!
> . . . .
> for I am God and not man,
>> the Holy One in your midst,
>> and I will not come to destroy.

The Good Friday story does not end with Jesus' cry of abandonment. The crucified man who continued to say "my God" could, in the end, commit his spirit into the keeping of his Father, as we must one day also do. But even now, because we know that the God of Israel kept faith with Jesus, the faithful Israelite, raising him to new life and making him the promise of new life for each of us . . . because we know that, we can make the whole of Psalm 22 our prayer. We can say to each other as the psalmist does:

I will tell of thy name to my brethren;
  in the midst of the congregation I will praise thee:
You who fear the LORD, praise him!
  all you sons of Jacob, glorify him,
  and stand in awe of him, all you sons of Israel!
For he has not despised or abhorred
  the affliction of the afflicted;
and he has not hid his face from him,
  but has heard, when he cried to him.

That is the deeper magic from before the dawn of time—the mystery of a God in whom, as St. Paul says, it is not yes and no. Rather, "in him it is always yes."

The Fifth Word (i)

"I thirst."

"I thirst," Jesus says.

But, of course, the dying are often thirsty. Is anything more ordinary than that? What we come to observe on this Good Friday is, therefore, nothing unusual. We see what human beings have often seen, what we ourselves may well have seen, what we ourselves may one day experience: that the dying are thirsty.

The bystanders around the cross—soldiers and others—could not, therefore, have been particularly surprised when Jesus says "I thirst." They seem even to have been prepared for it, having the sour wine there for just such a possibility.

But St. John does not intend us to see here only something ordinary and expected. No, for John it's clear that God is at work in what is happening, active in this crucifixion. So Jesus does not, in John's Gospel, say "I thirst" simply because he's a dying man and therefore naturally thirsts.

Jesus thirsts because everything is now finished, and the scriptures of Israel are being brought to their completion on this cross—a completion of the long story of God's own thirst. God's long, involved, convoluted plan, beginning with Abraham, to make of Israel a faithful people, a light to the nations—that plan now comes to its final act. Here at last is what God has been thirsting for all along—a truly faithful Israelite. And such a man must inevitably end on a cross, must be at cross purposes with a world that does not want to be formed and shaped in the ways of obedience and faithfulness.

So Jesus thirsts—because he is the faithful one for whom we have been waiting, the Israelite whom God provides. Jesus makes his own the prayer of Israel's psalmist

> *Save me, O God! . . .*
>
> *I am weary with my crying;*
>
> *my throat is parched. . . .*
>
> *and for my thirst they gave me vinegar to drink. . . .*
>
> *[But] I will praise the name of God with a song;*
>
> *I will magnify him with thanksgiving. . . .*
>
> *For the LORD hears the needy.*

The Lord hears the needy. Jesus thirsts not just because dying men thirst, but because God thirsts— thirsts for us. So Job, that great sufferer, says even in the midst of his suffering: "You will call, and I will answer you. You will long for the creature you have made."

God longs for us, the creature he has made for himself. Think of what that means for Christians on this Good Friday. We are no longer simply observers or onlookers. This is where we get invited into the story. The Almighty God, the One who made all that is, thirsts for you and for me. Thirsts with a desire so great that it brings him to this cross.

No matter how often Israel forgot her covenant with the LORD, he did not forget. "How can I give you up, O Israel," he says through the prophet Hosea. And Jesus himself, in one of his most unforgettable parables, pictures for us the waiting father—standing anxiously by the door, scanning the horizon for the return of his wayward son, thirsting to be reconciled with him and eager to celebrate his homecoming. We are invited into the story as those for whom God thirsts.

But we are also invited into this story in a second way—as those who are given the opportunity to quench Jesus' thirst. This is not the first time in John's Gospel that Jesus has been thirsty. Back in chapter 4, at Jacob's well in Samaria, he had asked a Samaritan woman to give him water to drink, and she had done so. She had—think of it—she had quenched God's thirst.

Where are the faithful ones here in John's crucifixion story? We're familiar, of course, with the presence of at least one of the disciples, and the women, and Jesus' mother Mary in particular, around the cross. But who runs to quench his thirst? John writes: "A jar full of sour wine stood there, so they put a sponge full of the sour wine on a hyssop branch and held it to his mouth."

Who are they—the ones who do this? Almost surely, the soldiers themselves. They had done their duty as executioners. They stood observing the three deaths. But when this dying man says he's thirsty, when they are invited to participate in a different way in his story, they do not miss their chance. They do not remain simply onlookers. They may not know exactly what they are doing. We may not know exactly what moves them to do it or whether they're really even trying to be of help. But—the fact is the fact—they quench God's thirst.

The question for us this Good Friday is whether we can measure up to the standard set by that Samaritan woman and these Roman soldiers. When, in a well-known passage in Matthew's Gospel, Jesus pictures the final judgment, he says to those who are to inherit the kingdom: "Come . . . for I was thirsty and you gave me drink." "When, Lord," they ask, "did we see you thirsty?"

"As you did it to one of the least of these my brothers, you did it to me," he replies.

Which is to say, day after day—not just today, but day after day—we are invited into this Good Friday story. Invited not just to be onlookers or observers at Jesus' cross but active participants who seek to quench his thirst. Like the Samaritan woman at the well, like these soldiers, we are to see in the thirsty faces of those around us the face of Jesus—the face of the God whose thirst for us is so great that he ends on this cross. Those faces all around us thirst for water, for peace, for help with the burdens they carry, for friendship, for freedom from the anxieties and demons that haunt them, for freedom to pursue their plans and projects—and, above all, they thirst to learn of the God who thirsts for them.

In this springtime it is no longer the bleak midwinter, but the words of the English Christmas carol by that name express as simply as can be how we should respond when invited into this story of the God who thirsts for us:

> *What can I give him, poor as I am?*
> *If I were a shepherd, I would bring a lamb.*
> *If I were a Wise Man, I would do my part;*
> *Yet what I can I give him: give my heart.*

The Fifth Word (ii)

"I thirst"

The fifth word of Jesus from the cross seems so ordinary, especially when we compare it with the word that comes just before it: "My God, my God, why have you forsaken me?" In that fourth word, we suspect, there are hidden mysteries and depths that could not fully be unpacked by the most profound of theologians: that God should be forsaken by God.

But, "I thirst"? This word, by contrast, seems all too ordinary. Pretty much the sort of thing we might expect from anyone near death from crucifixion. We would expect, as the psalmist says, that the crucified man's tongue would cleave to the roof of his mouth. And because this word is so ordinary, so expected, we have a harder time imagining that it might contain depths and mysteries beyond our reckoning. This we can understand.

Perhaps, then, we should begin there, begin with the ordinariness of physical suffering. We have not, of course, experienced the agonies of a man crucified, but we know what it is to be thirsty. Or hungry. We know what it is to suffer little aches and pains, to be stiff when you get up in the morning in a way you never were 20, or 30, or 40 years ago. We know what it is to have joints swell and ache, to lie sick in bed.

All that is ordinary enough, and we can push the ordinary yet a little further. Perhaps we have also known the deep, searing pain of serious physical injury. Or we have received a diagnosis of cancer, with its implication that, somehow, our own body has turned against us and become the enemy. Perhaps we have the terrifying suspicion that our ability to think clearly and remember may be starting to disintegrate. All this, alas, is still all too ordinary. But we thirst to be relieved of it—to be well, healthy, vigorous. When Jesus thirsts, therefore, he shares what is all too human, what we all know and experience in our own bodies in different ways.

But there is still more. For we also thirst in ways that are not, strictly speaking, just bodily. Indeed, our deepest thirsts are probably not those of the body. We thirst for love and companionship. For security—a sense that we are safe and cannot, finally, be harmed. We thirst for confidence that our work and our labor will not be in vain but will, in the end, amount to something. And we thirst for God, for the One whom our hearts are made to enjoy.

Important as the thirsts of the body are, how much deeper are these thirsts of the spirit. And when he says, "I thirst," Jesus shares them also. He longs to know that he has not been abandoned. He thirsts to know that somehow, in the midst of his agony, he is nonetheless safe and secure. He wants to know that, contrary to all the external evidence, what he is doing will not finally be in vain. He thirsts to know that even now, on a cross, he remains the beloved Son, still at one with his Father.

All this ordinary human thirst of body and spirit he suffers. But the One who suffers it is not ordinary.

This is not the first time in John's Gospel that Jesus has been thirsty. When in chapter four Jesus met a Samaritan woman at a well, the first thing he said to her was, "Give me a drink." Yet, it was not much later in that—to her—surprising conversation that he was offering her a drink of living water. "Whoever drinks of the water that I shall give him will never thirst."

Now, by the time we come to Calvary, in chapter nineteen of John's Gospel, the One who himself is living water thirsts. God thirsts. All those human thirsts of body and spirit that we know so well and experience every day as part of ordinary life, God here shares. They are taken into the divine life, the communion of Father and Son in the bond of the Spirit. This now is what God too is like—thirsty.

Richard Selzer is a surgeon well known also as an essayist who, from the angle of his medical practice, writes about life. In one of his essays he recounts an incident from his own practice, when he had operated on a young woman to remove a tumor from her cheek.

> I stand by the bed where a young woman lies, her face postoperative, her mouth twisted in palsy, clownish. A tiny twig of the facial nerve, the one to the muscles of the mouth, has been severed. She will be thus from now on. The surgeon had followed with religious fervor the curve of her flesh; I promise you that. Nevertheless, to remove the tumor in her cheek, I had to cut that little nerve.
>
> Her young husband is in the room. He stands on the opposite side of the bed, and together they seem to dwell in the evening lamplight, isolated from me. Who are they, I ask myself, he and this wry-mouth that I have made, who gaze at and touch each other so generously, greedily? The young woman speaks.
>
> "Will my mouth always be like this?" she asks. "Yes," I say, "it will. It is because the nerve was cut."

She nods and is silent. But the young man smiles. "I like it," he says. "It is kind of cute."

All at once I know who he is. I understand, and I lower my gaze. One is not bold in an encounter with a god. Unmindful, he bends to kiss her crooked mouth, and I so close I can see how he twists his own lips to accommodate to hers, to show her that their kiss still works.

Just so, when God on the cross thirsts. Bending down that his own lips may be parched and his tongue cleave to the roof of his mouth, to show us that he is still with us, thirsty as we are. And about that, about God doing that, there is nothing ordinary at all—is there? Your life and mine, all our thirsts—the tiny, piddling ones, and the ones so overpowering that they dominate our life—all are here drawn into God's own life and transformed into glory.

When, just a few verses later in John's Gospel, a soldier pierces with his spear the side of the now dead Jesus, there flows out blood and water. Here on Calvary's holy mountain we find the pure and healing fountain. This, it turns out, is the way you get living water. Only the God who knows thirst can quench thirst, and here he bends low to do so.

The Sixth Word (i)

"It is finished."

"It is finished," Jesus says. What's finished? Not just his life. Not just his suffering on the cross. What's finished is the entire task he has undertaken in agreement with his Father and in the power of their Spirit. That is the task of sharing our life to its very end, as our representative in the flesh. He has done that and done it faithfully in a way we ourselves could not.

John's Gospel depicts the arc of Jesus' life very simply: He came from his Father and returns to his Father—drawing us back to the God from whom we have turned away, making known to us what the Father has made known to him, sending the Spirit who binds him and his Father together in love in order to create here among us a community of love. And that work he now completes—finishes—on the cross, which, however strange it may seem to us, is in John's Gospel the place where Jesus' glory is seen, the glory he had with the Father from eternity.

When Jesus comes to Jerusalem for that last, fatal time, he does not do so blindly. He can see what is happening and can guess what plans the leaders of the people may be making. "And what shall I say?" he asks. "Father, save me from this hour? No, for this purpose I have come to this hour. Father, glorify thy name."

Christians sing a hymn called "In the cross of Christ I glory." We glory in it because that is where God shows his glory. We see here a very unusual God. If we Christians were not so accustomed to thinking about God in this way, we might be puzzled—or even, perhaps, offended. For this is not the way everyone thinks or has thought about God.

There is another famous story—no longer as famous as the story of Jesus on the cross, but, still, a story that as recently as, say, one hundred years ago every schoolchild would probably have known well. In what may be the most famous scene in Homer's *Iliad*, the aged Trojan king Priam comes to Achilles to plead for the body of his dead son, Hector, who has been slain by Achilles.

Achilles is a very hard man, but the sight of the old king begging for the body of his son moves Achilles to tears. Eventually both he and Priam together give way to their grief. But then Achilles says: We may as well stop these tears. There's no good to be gotten from them.

This is just the kind of life we wretched men have; it's only the gods who live free of sorrows.

Only the gods live free of sorrows. That vision of the gods is strikingly apparent a little earlier in the poem when Hector—still alive at that point—confronts Achilles, who is terrifying in his power and anger. Even Hector, himself a mighty warrior, is afraid. But the goddess Athena comes to Hector disguised as his brother Deiphobus, and promises to help him in the fight against Achilles.

So Hector takes heart, thanking Deiphobus (or the one he thinks is Deiphobus) for daring, as he puts it, "to venture out from the walls, all for my sake, while the others stay inside and cling to safety."

Hector confronts Achilles and hurls his spear, but it glances off Achilles' shield. Hector shouts to Deiphobus to bring him another spear, but, Homer says,

> *the man was nowhere near him, vanished—*
> *yes and Hector knew the truth in his heart.*
> *I thought he was at my side, the hero Deiphobus—*
> *he's safe inside the walls.*

Homer's tale is a stirring one that has demonstrated remarkable staying power for centuries. But how different is the god it depicts from the One on whose crucifixion we look today. the God who says from the cross, "it is finished." For the God of whom St. John writes, the God whose death Christians everywhere ponder today, is not a god who lives free of sorrows. Not a god who stays safe inside the city walls. On the contrary, this is a God who shares our place, our sorrow, our end—a God who is by our side upon the plain, as Luther's great hymn puts it.

If our lives often seem out of control, so did his often seem to be. If the plans we've made look as if they are coming to a bad end, so did his. If we've been tempted to wonder whether there is any point or purpose to the days of our lives, surely he was so tempted. If we feel ourselves weakening and the strength of life ebbing away from us, so did he. Yet, for all that, it's very clear in John's Gospel that "it is finished" is not a despairing cry but a triumphant one. It is triumphant because it is the cry of One who was faithful to the finish, to the very end.

We really had no reason or right to expect such a faithful God, one who is willing to live as our representative and follow that course to the finish. Nevertheless, the God we could neither expect nor demand is the God we need and the God we can love.

We're a bit like the little girl who was afraid of the dark. To calm her fear, her parents would always assure her at bedtime that God was watching over her. But one night, maybe an especially dark night, she called her mother back in, wanting her to stay with her, and she said: "Mommy, I know God's in here with me, but I need somebody with skin."

That is what we have in this God on the cross: somebody with skin, like us, with us, for us in the flesh to the finish.

In the cross of that God we see glory. And to that God who faithfully stood by us on a green hill far away outside the city wall until he could say "it is finished," we therefore say today: "for that last triumphant cry, we praise you evermore on high."

The Sixth Word (ii)

"It is finished."

Jesus says, "it's finished." And there are two obvious questions. What is finished? And what does it mean to say that it's finished?

Take first the question that looks easier. What is finished? Well, if we look at John's Gospel, the answer is clear: the work Jesus was sent to do is finished. When Jesus wonders whether he should ask his Father to save him from the hour that is coming, he concludes: "No, for this purpose I have come to this hour." When, a little later in the Gospel, Jesus prays for his disciples, he says to his Father, "I have accomplished the work you gave me to do."

So the first question—what is finished?—seems relatively straightforward, though we will have to circle back to it before we're done. How about the second question? What does it mean to say that this work is finished?

Ask the biblical scholars and they will tell you that in John's Gospel these words are a cry of victory. John is very clear that the hour when Jesus is lifted up on the cross is the hour of his glorification. Jesus himself, after he has washed the disciples' feet at the last supper, says, "Now is the Son of man glorified."

The Lenten hymn, "Christ the Life of All the Living," invites us to understand what is happening on the cross in this same way: as a triumph, a victory.

> *Then, for all that bought my pardon,*
> *For the sorrows deep and sore,*
> *For the anguish in the garden,*
> *I will thank you evermore;*
> *Thank you for the groaning, sighing,*
> *For the bleeding and the dying,*
> *For that last triumphant cry,*
> *Praise you evermore on high.*

So these words—"it is finished"—are a shout of triumph. No doubt that is true. But how can we hear that today, how hear in them the sound of victory? To hear Jesus' words that way we need to think a little longer about what it really means to say that something is finished. There are different ways in which some great work can reach its finish.

I have watched my wife "laboring," as we say, to give birth to a child. The labor seems to go on and on—and then, suddenly, it is finished. That end of that labor is new life—a finish that is fulfillment, completion, giving it point and making it worth doing. That is one kind of ending.

I have watched my father dying—"laboring," as we say, just to draw a breath near the end of life. That labor also seems to go on and on—and then, suddenly, it too is finished. He died, in fact, rather as his own father had, whose last words at the age of ninety-one were, *"Ich kann nicht mehr."* "I can't any longer." Both of them just wore out; they were finished. But where in that is any fulfillment that makes it all worthwhile, that makes it a victory? That labor just seems to end, and that's quite a different sort of finish.

If Jesus' finished work on the cross is fulfillment and victory, that is only because he dies with the hope that his father will not abandon him. The Father who once brought him forth from the womb of Mary will bring him forth again from the tomb into which he is laid. And so, for Jesus of Nazareth, the forces of evil are dealt a death blow. They are finished.

What about us—the work we're given to do, the lives we lead day after day on that relentless trajectory toward death? Can it be that the "labor" of our lives, which one day for us too may become the labor just to draw a breath . . . can it be that this "labor," when it is finished, has a point? An ending that is not just an end, but, rather, fulfillment and victory?

We would like that. We'd like it so much, in fact, we desire it so eagerly, that what we'd really like is to find a way to make it happen. We want to assure ourselves that our end will be not just an end but a fulfillment. We'd like not to have to live in hope. And that brings us back around to our first question: *What* is finished? Its answer seemed quite obvious and in many ways is obvious: What is finished is the work Jesus has been given to do.

Because that is true, it now turns out that something else is finished as well on this cross. Not only Jesus' work, but also the work we do to try to secure ourselves, to make happen what we want to happen. That's finished.

Jesus' words are a challenge to us today—a challenge to accept our limits, the limits to what we can accomplish. I cannot bring my life to an end that is fulfillment. The best I can manage on my own is an end that will look like my father's and my grandfather's. Laboring to draw a breath and, finally, unable to do so any longer. It'll just be finished.

I cannot bring my life to an end that is fulfillment. Nor can you. We want so badly to do that, but that's finished. That desire is put to death on the cross. Put to death so that we can learn with Jesus to live in hope, so that we can have a new image of what the "finish" of our life may be.

To the eyes of faith the laborings of our lives are enfolded within that great labor of the man on the cross. And faith gives rise to hope—hope that, in and through his labor, when we draw our last breath and say "it is finished," those words will mark not just an end, but a fulfillment and a victory.

The Seventh Word (i)

"Father, into your hands I commit my spirit."

Now I lay me down to sleep,
I pray thee, Lord, my soul to keep.
If I should die before I wake,
I pray thee, Lord, my soul to take.

We think of that as a child's bedtime prayer—and so it is. But then, of course, Jesus says that unless we become as little children, we will not enter the kingdom.

Many of us probably learned that simple prayer as children—often, I suspect, with one concluding line added: "And this I ask for Jesus' sake." And Jesus' own dying words on the cross may well be a prayer he himself had learned as a little Jewish boy, for he is simply quoting a line from the psalmist (31:5): "Into thy hand I commit my spirit."

As we seek—not just today on Good Friday, but every day—to let our lives be drawn into the story of Jesus' life, we ought to ask ourselves: How can I live so that, in my last breath, I am able to make Jesus' prayer my own? So that I too can say: "Father, into thy hands I commit my spirit."

This is not the first time Jesus had said essentially this. He said it as a twelve-year-old boy in the temple. He said it when he was tempted by Satan in the wilderness. He said it in his teaching—"consider the lilies; if your heavenly Father clothes them, how much more will he clothe you?" He said it when he went apart by himself, as he often did, to pray. He said it in Gethsemane—"not my will, but thine, be done."

And he says it now—on the cross, on Good Friday—after everything he has been given to do is finished. He can say it now because he has been saying it day after day, moment after moment, every day of his life. So must we.

I made progress today on an important piece of work.

Father, into thy hands I commit my spirit.

I read *Goodnight Moon* for the 18th time this week.

Father, into thy hands I commit my spirit.

I've raised a son who's about to graduate from college.

Father, into thy hands I commit my spirit.

I didn't get done what I told my friend I'd accomplish for her.

Father, into thy hands I commit my spirit.

I spent the afternoon in the dentist's chair.

Father, into thy hands I commit my spirit.

I spent the evening in conversation with old friends.

Father, into thy hands I commit my spirit.

I looked at the x-rays with the doctor and heard the diagnosis.

Father, into thy hands I commit my spirit.

Day by day we must practice this in things big and things small. Practice letting go and handing over what we have and who we are, handing it over to Jesus' Father for safekeeping. And then, with Jesus and in the power Jesus' Spirit gives, we will be able to say it one last time. We will have learned to enter the kingdom as a little child.

However much we may talk about the innocence or naiveté of youth, there's really nothing all that carefree about a child's existence. Children have problems and worries of their own.

So becoming as a little child does not mean being problem-free, carefree, or naive. It means practice: practicing time after time, learning day after day, to say what does not come naturally or easily to most children:

"Now I lay me down to sleep; I pray thee, Lord, my soul to keep."

Even seemingly carefree children sometimes have bad dreams. They cry out for help in the night. Their mother, or their father, comes into the bedroom and says, "don't worry; everything's all right."

What do you mean—everything's all right? I didn't get my assignments done. I got into trouble at school. My knee hurts where I scraped it. And I see some scary faces over there in the corner. What do you mean— everything's all right?

And just what do we mean? What—or Who—gives us the authority to say in that dark of night: "You may let go and hand over your cares and your fears. You may go to sleep. Everything—everything's all right.

It does not look as if everything's all right on that cross on Calvary. Indeed, it looks as if almost everything has gone wrong. Nevertheless, Jesus has finished the work of perfect obedience and sacrifice the Father had given him to do as our representative—the second Adam, the faithful Israelite. He has finished what had to be done and finished it in a way we never really manage to finish our own plans and projects. Now he lets go of all plans and projects. He says: "Now I lay me down to sleep; I pray thee, Lord, my soul to keep."

Everything's all right. And we too may let go. We may commit to Jesus' Father and our Father all that has gone well and all that has gone badly—and, perhaps especially, all that we have left unfinished and incomplete. We may do this because Jesus has finished his work for us and handed his life over to his Father. As one of the church's great evening hymns puts it:

> *Though bodies slumber,*
>
> *hearts shall keep their vigil,*
>
> *Forever resting*
>
> *in the peace of Jesus.*

And that is, after all, how we learned as little children—or should learn on this Good Friday—to close our evening prayer.

> *Now I lay me down to sleep,*
>
> *I pray thee, Lord, my soul to keep.*
>
> *If I should die before I wake,*
>
> *I pray thee, Lord, my soul to take.*
>
> *And this I ask for Jesus' sake. Amen.*

The Seventh Word (ii)

"Father, into your hands I commit my spirit."

For almost 1500 years Christians have, especially during Holy Week, sung the hymn called in Latin *Vexilla Regis prodeunt*, or in our English translation, "The Royal Banners Forward Go." The *vexilla* were the military standards and insignia carried ahead of kings into battle. But now, on Good Friday, the cross, that instrument of shame and torture, is the royal standard of the King of Kings.

Here at Calvary this king has finished the work God had promised to Israel of old, as the hymn says:

> *Fulfilled is all that David told*
> *In true prophetic song of old,*
> *That God the nations' king should be*
> *And reign in triumph from the tree.*

Reigning from that tree, Jesus does what he had once promised: Being lifted up, he draws all people to himself. And committing himself to his Father, he therefore commits us also.

Throughout his life Jesus had, as the Letter to the Hebrews says, learned the meaning of obedience. He had to learn what it meant to hold fast to Israel's God, and we know what a struggle that was when, for instance, he was tempted by Satan in the wilderness or had to struggle with the feeling of terror in Gethsemane. But now, having worked so hard to hold fast, he must learn the last and hardest lesson of all: to let go. To realize that the struggle is no longer his to undertake. To commit his spirit to his Father, trusting that the One who cared for the birds of the air and the lilies of the field would care for him even in the hour of death.

And therefore, on Good Friday, the church throughout the world prays that it too may learn such obedient trust. As the evenings of our life fade into the final evening of death, we must become like the musician who learns when to hold a note and when to let it slowly fade away into silence. That is the way of true wisdom.

Ours, however, is a world that often prefers power to wisdom. From medicine we want more than attempts to cure our ills and care for us when cure is unavailable; we want to enhance our natural capacities, to be "better than well," to make old age the last frontier to be conquered. From politics we want more than a peace that is, as St. Augustine put it, "the tranquility of order;" we want a world entirely freed from fear, a world in which there are no limits to the prosperity possible for us. From our work we want more than an honorable way of earning a living while serving the needs of others; we want a sense of accomplishment and fulfillment that makes our life complete.

In short, we want complete mastery in life, not the sense of incompletion that ends each day, each year, and finally each life, feeling that we're not yet ready to let go. It's not easy for us to let ourselves really be drawn into Jesus' final prayer—really to commit, to hand over, our spirit to God's keeping. For more almost than anything else we want a sense of completion in life: To finish the projects we undertake. To see our children and grandchildren. To go, as the title of one of E.B. White's essays puts it, "once more to the lake." To read one more book or listen to one more concert that we've not yet managed to do. To watch the flowers bloom another spring.

C.S. Lewis captured well this sense in his short poem, "What the Bird Said Early in the Year." It is inscribed on a memorial plaque near Addison's Walk at Magdalen College in Oxford.

I heard in Addison's Walk a bird sing clear
"This year the summer will come true. This year. This year.

"Winds will not strip the blossom from the apple trees
This year, nor want of rain destroy the peas.

"This year time's nature will no more defeat you,
Nor all the promised moments in their passing cheat you.

"This time they will not lead you round and back
To Autumn, one year older, by the well-worn track.

"This year, this year, as all these flowers foretell,
We shall escape the circle and undo the spell.

"Often deceived, yet open once again your heart,
Quick, quick, quick, quick! – the gates are drawn apart."

And yet, the gates always seem to slam shut before we can slip through, don't they? The completion we hoped to achieve and experience eludes us, as the promised moments in their passing cheat us. We cannot keep those gates from slamming shut, and we must learn to make Jesus' prayer our own. It takes practice.

Day by day we can say in the words of Luther's evening prayer: "Into your hands we commend our bodies and souls, and all that is ours. Let your holy angels have charge over us, that the wicked one have no power over us." And then one day, in the presence of our lifeless body, others can use Jesus' same prayer and say, as we do in the church's funeral rite: "Into your hands, O merciful Savior, we commend your servant. . . . Receive him into the arms of your mercy, into the blessed rest of everlasting peace, and into the glorious company of the saints in light."

And we have God's promise that such a prayer, when it is taken up into the prayer of Jesus, will not be in vain. For in what is God's own great mystery, relinquishing our hold on life, committing our spirit to the Father together with Jesus' own great act of relinquishing—turns out to be the secret to life.

Even today, then, as we gaze in wonder at the cross, we do so as those who, commending our spirits to Jesus' Father, can look toward Easter and see in that cross a tree of beauty, as the hymn says:

> O tree of beauty, tree most fair,
> Ordained those holy limbs to bear:
> Gone is your shame, each crimsoned bough
> Proclaims the King of glory now.

Made in the USA
Columbia, SC
26 January 2018